A BOOK OF PRAYER

Also by Peter Watkins & Erica Hughes

HERE'S THE CHURCH

HERE'S THE YEAR

A Book of Prayer

Compiled by

PETER WATKINS & ERICA HUGHES

Julia MacRae

A division of Franklin Watts

© in this collection 1982 Peter Watkins & Erica Hughes

All rights reserved
First published in Great Britain
Julia MacRae Books
A division of Franklin Watts
8 Cork Street, London, W1X 2HA
and Franklin Watts Inc.
387 Park Avenue South,
New York 10016.

Book designed by Douglas Martin
Printed in Great Britain by the Camelot Press, Southampton.

British Library Cataloguing in Publication Data

A Book of prayer.
  1. Prayer-books
  I. Watkins, Peter, *1934 –*   II. Hughes, Erica
  242'.8   BV245

ISBN 0–86203–108–7 UK edition
ISBN 0–531–04578–1 US edition
Library of Congress Catalog Card No. 82–60929

My words fly up, my thoughts remain below:
Words without thoughts never to heaven go.

William Shakespeare, *Hamlet* Act III, Scene 3

Contents

Introduction

In past generations children heard traditional prayers every day in school; the community heard them again in church on Sunday; and many families repeated them yet again in the privacy of their own homes.

Worship is often neglected in the schools of today; in many churches ugly modern translations and adaptations have replaced the magnificent liturgies of the past; family prayers now seem out of place in our informal style of living.

The loss is keenly felt by many. Is it already irreversible? The purpose of this book is to avert this dismal prospect. It collects together the best of prayers – the beautiful, the profound, the simple. It is not intended to be narrowly denominational, but prayers do not generally translate well from one language to another. We are therefore thrown heavily, and willingly, on to the resources of *The Book of Common Prayer* of 1662.

It is the fate of most prayer books to be placed on a shelf next to books of reference, and only rarely taken down. We hope that this book will be left lying around for all to browse in for their spirit's refreshment.

Supplications

. . . More things are wrought by prayer
Than this world dreams of.

Tennyson, *Idylls of the King*

Lord, teach us to pray

The Gospel of Luke, 2:1

THE LORD'S PRAYER

Pater noster,
qui es in coelis,
sanctificetur nomen tuum:
Adveniat regnum tuum.
Fiat voluntas tua,
sicut in coelo, et in terra.
Panem nostrum quotidianum da nobis hodie.
Et dimitte nobis debita nostra,
sicut et nos dimittimus debitoribus nostris;
Et ne nos inducas in tentationem,
sed libera nos a malo.

Our Father,
which art in heaven,
Hallowed be thy Name.
Thy kingdom come.
Thy will be done,
in earth as it is in heaven.
Give us this day our daily bread.
And forgive us our trespasses,
As we forgive them that trespass against us.
And lead us not into temptation;
But deliver us from evil.

Our Father which in Heaven art,
    We sanctify thy Name;
Thy Kingdom come, thy will be done,
    In Heaven and Earth the same.
Give us this day, our daily bread,
    And us forgive thou so,
As we on them that us offend,
    Forgiveness do bestow.
Into temptation lead us not,
    And us from evil free,
For thine the Kingdom, Power and Praise,
    Is and shall ever be.

George Wither, 1588–1667

Let the words of my mouth, and the meditation of my heart:
be alway acceptable in thy sight,
    O Lord: my strength, and my redeemer.

Psalm 19, 14–15

The prayers I make will then be sweet indeed
    If thou the spirit give by which I pray:
    My unassisted heart is barren clay,
That of its native self can nothing feed.

Michelangelo, 1475–1564

Good Lord, deliver us.
From all blindness of heart; from pride, vain-glory and hypocrisy;
from envy, hatred, and malice, and all uncharitableness;
From all sedition, privy conspiracy, and rebellion;
from all false doctrine, heresy, and schism;
from hardness of heart, and contempt of thy Word and Commandment.

By the mystery of thy holy Incarnation;
by thy holy Nativity and Circumcision;
by thy Baptism, Fasting and Temptation;
By thine Agony and bloody Sweat;
by thy Cross and Passion;
by thy precious Death and Burial;
by thy glorious Resurrection and Ascension;
and by the coming of the Holy Ghost,
Good Lord, deliver us.

We beseech thee to hear us, good Lord,
That it may please thee to give us an heart to love and dread thee,
and diligently to live after thy commandments;
That it may please thee to give to all thy people increase of grace
to hear meekly thy Word, and to receive it with pure affection,
and to bring forth the fruits of the Spirit,
That it may please thee to bring into the way of truth
all such as have erred, and are deceived,
That it may please thee to strengthen such as do stand;
and to comfort and help the weak-hearted;
and to raise up them that fall;
and finally to beat down Satan under our feet.

In all time of our tribulation;
in all time of our wealth;
in the hour of death, and in the day of judgement,
Good Lord, deliver us.

From the Litany of *The Book of Common Prayer*

Eyes to see – Ears to hear

Glory be to thee, O Lord,
for that thou didst create not only the visible light,
but the light invisible,
that which may be known of God, the law written in the heart;
give us a mind to perceive this light in
>the oracles of prophets,
>the melody of psalms,
>the prudence of proverbs,
>the experience of histories,
>and the life and love of our Lord Jesus Christ,
>for his sake.

Bishop Lancelot Andrewes, 1555–1626

God be in my head,
>And in my understanding;
God be in my eyes,
>And in my looking;
God be in my mouth,
>And in my speaking;
God be in my heart,
>And in my thinking;
God be at my end,
>And at my departing.

Old Sarum Primer, 1558

Speak, Lord, for thy servant heareth.
Grant us ears to hear,
Eyes to see,
Wills to obey,
Hearts to love;
Then declare what thou wilt,
Reveal what thou wilt,
Command what thou wilt,
Demand what thou wilt.

Christina Rossetti, 1830–94

[16]

Aspiration

Eternal God,
>the light of the minds that know thee,
>the joy of the hearts that love thee,
>the strength of the wills that serve thee.

Grant us,
>so to know thee that we may truly love thee,
>so to love thee that we may fully serve thee,
>whom to serve is perfect freedom.

The Gelasian Sacramentary

Help us, O God,
to serve thee devoutly
and the world busily.
May we do our work wisely,
give succour secretly,
go to our meat appetitely,
sit thereat discreetly,
arise temperately,
please our friend duly,
go to our bed merrily
and sleep surely,
for the joy of our Lord Jesus Christ.

Adaptation of a translation from Sulpicius,
printed by Wynkyn de Worde in 1500

Lord,
when we are wrong, make us willing to change,
and when we are right, make us easy to live with.

Peter Marshall, 1902–49

God grant me
The serenity to accept the things I cannot change,
The courage to change the things I can,
And the wisdom to distinguish the one from the other.

Reinhold Niebuhr, 1893–1971

Let the Eternal God be the portion of my soul;
let Heaven be my inheritance and hope;
let Christ be my Head, and my promise of security;
let Faith be my wisdom,
and Love my very Heart and Will,
and patient persevering Obedience be my life;
and then I can spare the wisdom of the world,
because I can spare the trifles that it seeks,
and all that they are like to get by it.

Richard Baxter, 1615–91

Lord,
let thy glory be my end,
thy word my rule,
and then thy will be done.

King Charles II, 1630–85

Addressed to Christ

Anima Christi, sanctifica me.
Corpus Christi, salva me,
Sanguis Christi, inebria me.
Aqua lateris Christi, lava me.
Passio Christi, conforta me.
O bone Jesu, exaudi me.
Intra tua vulnera absconde me.
Ne permittas me separari a te.
Ab hoste maligno defende me.
In hora mortis meae voca me.
Et jube me venire ad te,
Ut cum Sanctis tuis laudem te
In saecula saeculorum.

Soul of Christ, be my sanctification;
Body of Christ, be my salvation;
Blood of Christ, fill all my veins;
Water of Christ's side, wash out my stains;
Passion of Christ, my comfort be;
O good Jesu, listen to me:
In thy wounds I fain would hide,
Ne'er to be parted from thy side;
Guard me, should the foe assail me;
Call me when my life shall fail me,
Bid me come to thee above,
With thy saints to sing thy love
World without end. Amen.

Translated by Cardinal Newman, 1801–90

O Christ who holds the open gate,
O Christ who drives the furrow straight,
O Christ, the plough, O Christ, the laughter
Of holy white birds flying after,
Lo, all my heart's field red and torn,
And Thou wilt bring the young green corn
The young green corn divinely springing,
The young green corn for ever singing;
And when the field is fresh and fair
Thy blessèd feet shall glitter there.
And we will walk the weeded field,
And tell the golden harvest's yield,
The corn that makes the holy bread
By which the soul of man is fed,
The holy bread, the food unpriced,
Thy everlasting mercy, Christ.

John Masefield, 1878–1967, *The Everlasting Mercy*

For Strength and Protection

Be Lord,
within me to strengthen me,
without me to preserve me,
over me to shelter me,
beneath me to support me,
before me to divert me,
behind me to bring me back,
and round about me to fortify me.

Bishop Lancelot Andrewes, 1555–1626

Grant, O Lord,
that Christ himself may be formed in us,
that we may be conformable to his image;
for his name's sake.

Bishop Lancelot Andrewes, 1555–1626

Let me not pray to be sheltered from dangers,
    but to be fearless in facing them.
Let me not beg for the stilling of my pain,
    but for the heart to conquer it.
Let me not look for allies in life's battlefield,
    but to my own strength.
Let me not crave in anxious fear to be saved,
    but hope for the patience to win my freedom.
Grant me that I may not be a coward,
    feeling your mercy in my success alone;
    but let me find the grasp of your hand in my failure.

Rabindranath Tagore, 1861–1941

This is my prayer to thee, my lord –
    strike, strike at the root of penury in my heart.
Give me the strength lightly to bear my joys and sorrows.
Give me the strength never to disown the poor
    or bend my knees before insolent might.
Give me the strength to raise my mind high above daily trifles.
And give me the strength to surrender my strength
    to thy will with love.

Rabindranath Tagore, 1861–1941

O God our Father,
    let us not be content to wait and see what will happen,
    but give us the determination to make the right things happen.
While time is running out,
    Save us from patience which is akin to cowardice.
Give us the courage to be either hot or cold,
    to stand for something,
    lest we fall for anything.
        In Jesus' name. Amen.

Peter Marshall, 1902–49, Chaplain to U.S. Congress
(used in the Senate, 10 March 1948)

        Protégez-moi, mon Seigneur;
        mon navire est si petit,
        et votre mer est si grande.

        A traditional French prayer

[21]

In Time of Doubt

Take not thy Holy Spirit from us.

When thou wast taken, Lord, I oft have read,
All thy disciples thee forsook, and fled.
Let their example not a pattern be
For me to fly, but now to follow thee.

Robert Herrick, 1591–1674

O Lord Jesus Christ,
 who art the way, the truth, and the life,
we pray thee suffer us not to stray from thee who art the way,
nor to distrust thee who art the truth,
nor to rest in any other thing than thee who art the life.

Almighty God,
teach us by thy holy Spirit,
 what to believe,
 what to do,
 and wherein to take our rest.

Erasmus, 1466–1536

For Special Endeavours

O God,
who hast ordained that whatever is to be desired
should be sought by labour,
and who, by thy blessing, bringest honest labour to good effect:
look with mercy upon our studies and endeavours:
Grant us, O Lord, to desire only what is lawful and right,
that in humility of mind we may seek the truth,
and in gentleness of heart may we serve our generation.

Samuel Johnson, 1709–84

Grant, O merciful God, that
with malice towards none,
with charity to all,
with forgiveness in the right as thou givest us to see the right,
we may strive to finish the work we are in;
to bind up the nation's wounds,
to care for him who shall have borne the battle
and for his widow and orphan;
to do all which may achieve a just and lasting peace
among ourselves and with all nations.

Adapted from the words of Abraham Lincoln, 1809–65

O Lord God,
when Thou givest to Thy servants to endeavour any great matter,
grant us also to know that it is not the beginning
but the continuing of the same until it be thoroughly finished
which yieldeth the true glory.

Sir Francis Drake, c. 1540–96

Almighty Father
ruler of the elements and maker of the Universe in its tremendous majesty,
who hast filled men with the spirit of adventure,
and given them the desire to know more of thy creation;
grant us the power to live and work for thee that,
so forgetting self, we may do all to thy glory,
and bring to our fellow men a fuller realization of the wonder of thy Presence
which is in all, and through all, and over all;
through Jesus Christ our Lord.

This prayer was written for the explorers who went to the Antarctic in 1934

For the Church

Endue thy Ministers with righteousness.

Deus,
qui omnes homines vis salvos fieri,
et ad agnitionem veritatis venire;
mitte, quaesumus,
operarios in messem tuam,
et da eis cum omni fiducia loqui verbum tuum,
ut sermo tuus currat,
et clarificetur,
et omnes gentes cognoscant te
solum Deum verum,
et quem misisti
Jesum Christum
Filium tuum Dominum nostrum.

O God,
who willest that all men should be saved,
and come to the knowledge of the truth;
send forth, we beseech thee,
labourers into thy harvest,
and grant them grace to speak thy word with all boldness,
so that thy word may run
and be glorified,
and all nations may know thee,
the only true God,
and him whom thou hast sent,
even Jesus Christ,
thy Son, our Lord.

The Daily Missal

Jesus, good shepherd, they are not mine but yours,
for I am not mine but yours,
I am yours, Lord, and they are yours,
because by your wisdom you have created
both them and me,
and by your death you have redeemed us.
So we are yours, good Lord, we are yours,
whom you have made with such wisdom
and bought so dearly.
Then if you commend them to me, Lord,
you do not therefore desert me or them.
You commend them to me:
I commend myself and them to you.
Yours is the flock, Lord, and yours is the shepherd.
Be shepherd of both your flock and shepherd.

You have made an ignorant doctor, a blind leader,
An erring ruler:
teach the doctor you have established,
guide the leader you have appointed,
govern the ruler that you have approved.
I beg you,
teach me what I am to teach,
lead me in the way that I am to lead,
rule me so that I may rule others.
Or rather, teach them, and me through them,
lead them, and me with them,
rule them, and me among them.

Anselm, 1033–1109 (Archbishop of Canterbury 1093–1109), *Prayer by a Bishop
for the Members of His Church*, translated by Sister Benedicta Ward, S.L.G.,
used at Inauguration of Archbishop of Canterbury, 25 March 1980

When mothers with adoring eyes
Bring babies to the baptistry.
And place them in these arms of mine,
     Christ of Bethlehem, look on me.

When boys come running down the street
And take my arms in intimacy,
And humble me with trustful love,
     Christ of Nazareth, look on me.

When I go tramping over hills
That look towards the starlight sea
Under a sky of windy clouds,
     Christ of Emmaus, walk with me.

When at thy holy table, Lord,
I handle the good mystery
With these unworthy hands of mine,
     Christ of the Upper Room, remember me.

When in the room of death I stand
To solace pain and to set free
The labouring hearts of dying men,
     Christ of Calvary, strengthen me.

When at last I come to pay
The price of my mortality
When Sister Death shall close my eyes,
     Christ on the Throne, acknowledge me.

The Prayer of a Priest, anon.

     Almighty and everlasting God,
who alone workest great marvels:
Send down upon our Bishops, and Curates,
and all Congregations committed to their charge,
the healthful Spirit of thy grace;
and that they may truly please thee,
pour upon them the continual dew of thy blessing,
     Grant this, O Lord,
for the honour of our Advocate and Mediator, Jesus Christ.

The Book of Common Prayer

[27]

Universal Prayers

To God belongeth the east and west;
therefore whithersoever ye turn yourselves to pray,
there is the face of God.
To him belongeth whatever is in heaven and on earth;
and when he decreeth a thing he only saith unto it,
    Be,
and it is.

From the *Koran*

Whether the highest Being is called Visnu or Siva,
Brahma or Indra, Sun or Moon,
Buddha – the Enlightened, or Mahavir – the Perfect,
I always offer my salutations to Him alone who is free from
attachment and hatred,
worldliness and ignorance,
who is endowed with compassion towards all creatures,
and is possessed of all noble attributes.

Swami Yatiswarananda, *Universal Prayers*

In the name of Allah, the Beneficent, the Merciful.
Praise be to Allah, Lord of the Worlds,
the Beneficent, the Merciful,
Ruler of the Day of Judgement,
Thee do we worship;
Thee do we ask for help.
Show us the straight path,
the path of those whom thou hast favoured;
not of those who have earned thine anger,
nor of those who go astray.

From the first *Sura*, or chapter, of the *Koran*

Allah akbar
Ashhad a
La illah illa llah
we Muhammed rasul Allah
hayya ila s-salat
hayya il l-fehah
es-salet kher min en-num
Allah abbar
la llah illa llah

God is greatest
I testify that
there is no God save God
and that Mohammed is the apostle of God
Up to prayer
Up to salvation
Prayer is better than sleep
God is greatest
There is no God but God

The Islamic Call to Prayer

O my Lord!
If I worship thee from fear of hell,
      burn me in hell;
and if I worship thee from hope of Paradise,
      exclude me thence;
but if I worship thee for thine own sake,
      then withhold not from me thine Eternal Beauty.

An ancient Muslim prayer

O Lord,
grant us to love thee;
grant that we may love those who love thee;
grant that we may do the deeds that win thy love.
Make the love of thee to be dearer to us than
ourselves, our families, than wealth,
and even than cool water.

Mohammed, c. 570–632

[29]

God made the rivers to flow.
They feel no weariness, they cease not from flowing.
They fly swiftly like birds in the air.

May the stream of my life flow into the river of righteousness.
Loose the bonds of sin that tie me.
Let not the thread of my song be cut while I sing;
and let not my work end before its fulfilment.

From the *Bhagavad Gita*

From the unreal lead me to the real!
From darkness lead me to light!
From death lead me to immortality!

A Hindu prayer in the *Brihadaranyaka Upanishad*

O Lord our Saviour,
who hast warned us that thou wilt require much
of those to whom much is given;
grant that we whose lot is cast in so goodly a heritage
may strive together more abundantly
by prayer and by every other means
to extend to others what we so richly enjoy,
that as we have entered into the labours of other men,
we may so labour that others in their turn may enter into ours,
to the fulfilment of thy holy will.

A fourth-century prayer

O God,
who hast made of one blood all nations of men
for to dwell on the face of the earth,
and didst send thy blessed Son, Jesus Christ,
to preach peace to them that are afar off,
and to them that are nigh;
grant that all the peoples of the world
may feel after thee and find thee;
and hasten, O God, the fulfilment of thy promise,
to pour out thy spirit upon all flesh;

Bishop Cotton of Calcutta, 1813–66

For Peace

Give peace in our time, O Lord.

O God, make us children of quietness and heirs of peace.
Amen.

St Clement, first century

Almighty God,
from whom all thoughts of truth and peace proceed,
kindle, we pray thee, in the hearts of all men,
the true love of peace,
and guide with thy pure and peaceable wisdom
those who take counsel for the nations of the earth;
that in tranquillity thy kingdom may go forward,
till the earth be filled with the knowledge of thy love;
through Jesus Christ our Lord.

Francis Paget, 1851–1911

Drop thy still dews of quietness,
Till all our strivings cease:
Take from our souls the strain and stress,
And let our ordered lives confess
The beauty of thy peace.

John Greenleaf Whittier, 1807–92

For Simplicity

Pray God, keep us simple.

W.M. Thackeray, 1811–63

Teach us Delight in simple things,
And Mirth that hath no bitter springs:
Forgiveness free of evil done,
And Love to all men 'neath the sun!

Rudyard Kipling, 1865–1936,
'The Children's Song' from *Puck of Pook's Hill*

We offer in simplicity
   our loving gift and labour;
And what we do, we do to thee,
   incarnate in our neighbour.

Giles Ambrose, twentieth century

Lord, temper with tranquillity our manifold activity,
That we may do our work for Thee with very great simplicity.

A sixteenth-century prayer

Lord, that I may learn of Thee,
Give me true simplicity;
Wean my soul, and keep it low,
Willing Thee alone to know.

An eighteenth-century hymn verse

Prayers of the Saints

Almighty God,
who hast given us grace with one accord
to make our common supplications unto thee;
and dost promise that when two or three are gathered together in thy Name,
thou wilt grant their requests:
fulfil now, O Lord, the desires and petitions of thy servants,
as may be most expedient for them;
granting us in this world knowledge of thy Truth,
and in the World to come life everlasting.

St John Chrysostom, c. 345–407

O thou, from whom to be turned is to fall,
    to whom to be turned is to rise,
    and in whom to stand is to abide for ever;
Grant us in all our duties thy help,
    in all our perplexities thy guidance,
    in all our dangers thy protection,
    and in all our sorrows thy peace;
        through Jesus Christ our Lord.

Thou awakest us to delight in thy praise;
    for thou madest us for thyself,
    and our heart is restless,
    until it finds rest in thee.

Late have I loved thee,
    O Beauty so ancient and so new;
late have I loved thee!

Three prayers of St Augustine, 345–430

May the strength of God pilot us.
May the power of God preserve us.
May the wisdom of God instruct us.
May the hand of God protect us.
May the way of God direct us.
May the shield of God defend us.
May the host of God guard us
against the snares of evil and the temptations of the world.
May Christ be with us, Christ before us, Christ in us, Christ over us.
May thy salvation, O Lord,
be always ours this day and for evermore.

Attributed to St Patrick, c. 385–461, *St Patrick's Breastplate*

O gracious and holy Father,
Give us wisdom to perceive thee,
 intelligence to understand thee,
 diligence to seek thee,
 patience to wait for thee,
 eyes to behold thee
 a heart to meditate upon thee,
 and a life to proclaim thee;
through the power of the Spirit of Jesus Christ our Lord.

St Benedict, c. 480–547

O Lord our God,
 grant us grace to desire thee with our whole heart;
that, so desiring, we may seek,
 and seeking, find thee;
and so finding thee, may love thee;
and loving thee, may hate those sins
 from which thou hast redeemed us.

St Anselm, 1033–1109

Lord, make me an instrument of Thy peace:
    Where there is hatred, let me sow love;
    Where there is injury, pardon;
    Where there is discord, union;
    Where there is doubt, faith;
    Where there is despair, hope;
    Where there is darkness, light;
    Where there is sadness, joy.
O Divine Master, grant that I may not so much seek
    To be consoled as to console;
    To be understood as to understand;
    To be loved as to love;
    For it is in giving that we receive;
    It is in pardoning that we are pardoned;
    And it is in dying that we are born to eternal life.

St Francis of Assisi, c. 1181–1226

God of all goodness,
grant us to desire ardently,
to seek wisely,
to know surely,
and to accomplish perfectly thy holy will,
for the glory of thy name.

Give me, O Lord,
a steadfast heart,
which no unworthy thought can drag downwards;
an unconquered heart
which no tribulation can wear out;
an upright heart,
which no unworthy purpose may tempt aside.

Two prayers of St Thomas Aquinas, c. 1225–74

Teach us, good Lord,
to serve Thee as Thou deservest:
to give and not to count the cost;
to fight and not to heed the wounds;
to toil and not to seek for rest;
to labour and not to ask for any reward
save that of knowing that we do Thy will.

St Ignatius of Loyola, 1491–1556

Confessions and Absolutions

Ye that do truly and earnestly repent you of your sins,
and are in love and charity with your neighbours,
and intend to lead a new life, following the commandments of God,
and walking from henceforth in his holy ways;
Draw near with faith, and take this holy Sacrament to your comfort;
and make your humble confession to Almighty God,
meekly kneeling upon your knees.

From the Order for Holy Communion in *The Book of Common Prayer*

Dearly beloved brethren,
the Scripture moveth us in sundry places
to acknowledge and confess our manifold sins and wickedness;
and that we should not dissemble nor cloke them
before the face of Almighty God our heavenly Father;
but confess them with an humble, lowly, penitent and obedient heart;
to the end that we may obtain forgiveness of the same,
by his infinite goodness and mercy.

And although we ought at all times humbly to acknowledge our sins before God;
yet ought we most chiefly so to do, when we assemble and meet together
to render thanks for the great benefits that we have received at his hands,
to set forth his most worthy praise,
to hear his most holy Word,
and to ask those things which are requisite and necessary,
as well for the body as the soul.

Wherefore I pray and beseech you, as many as are here present,
to accompany me with a pure heart and humble voice
unto the throne of the heavenly grace.

From the Order of Morning Service in *The Book of Common Prayer*

Confiteor Deo omnipotenti,
et omnibus Sanctis,
quia peccavi nimis cogitatione,
verbo et opere,
mea culpa,
mea culpa,
mea maxima culpa.

I confess to Almighty God,
and to all the saints,
that I have sinned exceedingly in thought
word and deed,
through my fault,
through my fault,
through my most grievous fault.

The Daily Missal

Almighty and most merciful Father,
We have erred, and strayed from thy ways like lost sheep.
We have followed too much the devices and desires of our own hearts,
We have offended against thy holy laws,
We have left undone those things which we ought to have done,
And we have done those things which we ought not to have done,
And there is no health in us:
But thou, O Lord, have mercy upon us miserable offenders;
Spare thou them, O God, which confess their faults,
Restore thou them that are penitent,
According to thy promises declared unto mankind in Christ Jesu our Lord:
And grant, O most merciful Father, for his sake,
That we may hereafter live a godly, righteous, and sober life,
To the glory of thy holy Name.

The Public Confession at Morning and Evening Prayer in *The Book of Common Prayer*

All that we ought to have thought and have not thought,
All that we ought to have said and have not said,
All that we ought to have done and have not done;
All that we ought not to have thought and yet have thought,
All that we ought not to have spoken and yet have spoken,
All that we ought not to have done and yet have done;
>   For these words and works, we pray, O God
>   For forgiveness,
>   And we repent with penance.

This prayer is from the *Zendavesta,*
and it is ascribed to Zoroaster about 1500 BC

No deeds I've done nor thoughts I've thought;
Save as thy servant, I am naught.

Guard me, O God, and O, control
The tumult of my restless soul.

Ah, do not, do not cast on me
The guilt of my iniquity.

My countless sins, I, Tuka say,
Upon thy loving heart I lay.

Tukaram, 1607–49, A Hindu Confession

Jesus Christ, have mercy on me,
>   As thou art king of majesty;
And forgive my sins all
That I have done, both great and small;
And bring me, if it be thy will
To heaven to dwell aye with thee still.

Richard Rolle, 1290–1349

Wilt Thou forgive that sin, where I begun,
Which was my sin, though it were done before?
Wilt Thou forgive that sin, through which I run,
And do run still, though still I do deplore?
When Thou hast done, Thou hast not done;
    For I have more.

Wilt Thou forgive that sin which I have won
Others to sin, and made my sins their door?
Wilt Thou forgive that sin which I did shun
A year or two, but wallow'd in a score?
When Thou hast done, Thou hast not done;
    For I have more.

I have a sin of fear, that when I've spun
My last thread, I shall perish on the shore;
But swear by Thyself that at my death Thy Son
Shall shine, as He shines now and heretofore:
And, having done that, Thou hast done:
    I fear no more.

John Donne, 1572–1631, *A Hymn to God the Father*

Etienne de Vignolles, commonly called La Hire, 'the Growler', had little time to spare when he went to the relief of Montargis in 1427. He confessed to a priest that he had done all that a soldier usually did. He was absolved by the priest, and then he knelt by the roadside and prayed:

I pray my God to do for La Hire what La Hire would do for Him, if He were Captain and La Hire was God.

Almighty God, our heavenly Father,
who of his great mercy hath promis_d forgiveness of sins
to all them that with hearty repentance and true faith turn unto him;
Have mercy upon you;
pardon and deliver you from all your sins;
confirm and strengthen you in all goodness;
and bring you to everlasting life;
through Jesus Christ our Lord. Amen.

The Absolution from the Holy Communion in *The Book of Common Prayer*

May the almighty and merciful Lord
grant you pardon and remission of all your sins,
time for amendment of life,
and the grace and comfort of the Holy Spirit. Amen.

The Absolution in an Order for Compline

Words on our Way

There are Church ceremonies or sacraments to mark our way from the cradle to the grave. Prayers are said when we are christened, confirmed, married and buried at Baptisms, Confirmations, Weddings and Funerals.

Words at a Baptism

Almighty and everlasting God,
we beseech thee, that thou wilt mercifully look upon this child, that he
being steadfast in faith,
joyful through hope,
and rooted in charity,
may so pass the waves of this troublesome world,
that finally he may come to the land of everlasting life,
there to reign with thee world without end;
through Jesus Christ our Lord.

Adapted from *The Book of Common Prayer*

We receive this child into the Congregation of Christ's flock,
and do sign him with the sign of the Cross,
in token that hereafter he shall not be ashamed to confess
the faith of Christ crucified,
and manfully to fight under his banner
against sin, the world, and the devil,
and to continue Christ's faithful soldier and servant
unto his life's end.

From the Order of Baptism in *The Book of Common Prayer*

Almighty God, our heavenly Father,
whose blessed son did share at Nazareth the life and a home;
bless the home of this child,
and grant wisdom and understanding
to all who have the care of him;
that he may grow up to worship and love thee
in word and in deed.

The Book of Common Prayer, 1928

Lord Jesus Christ, our Lord most dear,
    As thou wast once an infant here,
So give this child of mine we pray,
Thy grace and heavenly blessing day by day.
        O Holy Jesus, Lord Divine,
        We pray thee, guard this child of mine.

A fifteenth-century German hymn

Words at a Confirmation

Defend, O Lord, this thy Child with thy heavenly grace,
    that he may continue thine for ever;
    and daily increase in thy Holy Spirit more and more,
    until he come unto thy everlasting Kingdom.

From the Order of Confirmation in *The Book of Common Prayer*

Words at a Wedding

Wilt thou have this Woman to thy wedded wife,
to live together after God's ordinance
in the holy estate of Matrimony?

Wilt thou love her, comfort her, honour,
and keep her, in sickness and in health;
and, forsaking all other,
keep thee only unto her, so long as ye both shall live?

The Man shall answer, 'I will'.

The Woman, with her right hand taking the Man by his right hand
    shall say:

I   N.   take thee   N.   to my wedded husband,
to have and to hold from this day forward,
for better for worse,
for richer for poorer,
in sickness and in health,
to love, cherish, and to obey,
    till death us do part,
according to God's holy ordinance;
and thereto I give thee my troth.

The Man, holding the Ring on the fourth finger
of the Woman's left hand, shall say:

With this Ring I thee wed,
with my body I thee worship,
and with all my worldly goods I thee endow:
    In the Name of the Father,
    and of the Son,
    and of the Holy Ghost. Amen.

From the Form of Solemnization of Matrimony in *The Book of Common Prayer*

Blessed art thou, O Lord our God, King of the universe,
who hast created joy and gladness, bride and bridegroom,
mirth and exultation, pleasure and delight,
love, brotherhood, peace and fellowship . . .
Blessed art thou, O Lord,
who makest the bridegroom to rejoice with the bride.

From the Benediction at the Wedding Service in *The Hebrew Prayer Book*

Almighty God,
who at the beginning did create our first parents, Adam and Eve,
and did sanctify and join them together in marriage;
Pour upon you the riches of his grace,
sanctify and bless you,
that ye may please him both in body and soul,
and live together in holy love unto your lives' end.

A prayer for the bride and bridegroom from *The Book of Common Prayer*

Words at a Death

O Father of all,
we pray to thee for those whom we love, but see no longer.
Grant them thy peace;
let light perpetual shine upon them,
and in thy loving wisdom and almighty power
work in them the good purpose of thy perfect will,
through Jesus Christ our Lord.

We give them back to thee, dear Lord,
Who gavest them to us.
Yet as thou dost not lose them in giving,
So we have not lost them by their return.
Not as the world givest, givest thou, O Lover of Souls.
When thou givest, thou takest not away.
For what is thine is ours always, if we are thine.
A life is eternal and love is immortal,
And death is only an horizon,
And an horizon is nothing save the limit of our sight.

Bring us, O Lord God,
at our last awakening into the house and gate of heaven,
to enter into that gate and dwell in that house,
where there shall be no darkness nor dazzling,
    but one equal light;
no noise nor silence,
    but one equal music;
no fears nor hopes,
    but one equal possession;
no ends nor beginnings,
    but one equal eternity;
in the habitations of thy glory and dominion world without end.

John Donne, 1572–1631

[51]

Even such is Time, that takes in trust
Our youth, our joys, our all we have,
And pays us but with earth and dust;
Who in the dark and silent grave,
When we have wandered all our ways
Shuts up the story of our days;
But from this earth, this grave, this dust,
My God shall raise me up, I trust.

These lines were written by Sir Walter Raleigh,
c. 1552–1618, on the fly-leaf of his Bible on the night before
he was executed at the Tower of London.

Forasmuch as it hath pleased Almighty God of his great mercy
to take unto himself the soul of our dear brother here departed,
we therefore commit his body to the ground; earth to earth,
ashes to ashes, dust to dust; in sure and certain hope of the
Resurrection to eternal life, through our Lord Jesus Christ.

From the Order for the Burial of the Dead in *The Book of Common Prayer*

Words of the Mass or Holy Communion

A Mass or Communion or Eucharist is as carefully constructed as a poem or play. All the words in this section come from either *The Book of Common Prayer* or *The Daily Missal*. They have been arranged with consideration for when they would be spoken during the Sacrament.

The Collect for Purity

Almighty God,
unto whom all hearts be open,
all desires known,
and from whom no secrets are hid:
Cleanse the thoughts of our hearts by the inspiration of thy Holy Spirit,
that we may perfectly love thee,
and worthily magnify thy holy Name;
through Christ our Lord.

Kyrie Eleison,	Lord have mercy,
Christe Eleison,	Christ have mercy,
Kyrie Eleison.	Lord have mercy.

The Gloria

Glory be to God on high,
and in earth peace, good will towards men.
We praise thee, we bless thee, we worship thee, we glorify thee,
we give thanks to thee for thy great glory,
O Lord God, heavenly King, God the Father Almighty.
O Lord, the only-begotten Son Jesu Christ;
O Lord God, Lamb of God, Son of the Father,
That takest away the sins of the world,
have mercy upon us.
Thou that takest away the sins of the world,
receive our prayer.
Thou that sittest at the right hand of God the Father,
have mercy upon us.
For thou only art holy;
thou only art the Lord;
thou only, O Christ, with the Holy Ghost,
art most high in the glory of God the Father. Amen.

[55]

The Credo

Credo in unum Deum,
Patrem omnipotentem,
Factorem coeli et terrae,
Visibilium omnium, et invisibilium
Et in unum Dominum Jesum Christum,
Filium Dei unigenitum,
Et ex Patre natum
ante omnia saecula,
Deum de Deo, lumen de lumine,
Deum verum de Deo vero,
Genitum, non factum,
consubstantialem Patri:
per quem omnia facta sunt.
Qui propter nos homines,
et propter nostram salutem
descendit de coelis,
Et incarnatus est de Spiritu Sancto
ex Maria Virgine:
et homo factus est.
Crucifixus etiam pro nobis:
sub Pontio Pilato
passus et sepultus est.
Et resurrexit tertia dei,
secundum Scripturas.
Et ascendit in coelum:
sedet ad dexteram Patris.
Et iterum venturus est cum gloria
judicare vivos, et mortuos:
cujus regni non erit finis.
Et in Spiritum Sanctum
Dominum et vivificantem:
qui ex Patre: Filioque procedit.
Qui cum Patre et Filio
simul adoratur, et conglorificatur:
qui locutus est per Prophetas.
Et unam sanctam catholicam
et apostolicam Ecclesiam.
Confiteor unum baptisma
in remissionem peccatorum.
Et exspecto resurrectionem mortuorum.
Et vitam venturi saeculi.
Amen.

or Creed

I believe in one God
the Father Almighty,
Maker of heaven and earth,
And of all things visible and invisible:
And in one Lord Jesus Christ,
the only-begotten Son of God,
Begotten of his Father
before all worlds,
God of God, Light of Light,
Very God of very God,
Begotten, not made,
Being of one substance with the Father,
By whom all things were made:
Who for us men
and for our salvation
came down from heaven,
And was incarnate by the Holy Ghost
of the Virgin Mary,
And was made man,
And was crucified also for us
under Pontius Pilate.
He suffered and was buried,
And the third day he rose again
according to the Scriptures,
And ascended into heaven,
And sitteth on the right hand of the Father.
And he shall come again with glory
to judge both the quick and the dead:
Whose kingdom shall have no end.
And I believe in the Holy Ghost,
The Lord and giver of life,
Who proceedeth from the Father and the Son,
Who with the Father and the Son
together is worshipped and glorified,
Who spake by the Prophets.
And I believe one Catholick
and Apostolick Church.
I acknowledge one Baptism
for the remission of sins.
And I look for the Resurrection of the dead,
And the life of the world to come.
Amen.

The Sursum Corda

Priest: Lift up your hearts.
Answer: We lift them up unto the Lord.
Priest: Let us give thanks unto our Lord God.
Answer: It is meet and right so to do.

The Sanctus

Sanctus, Sanctus, Sanctus,
Dominus Deus Sabaoth.
Pleni sunt coeli, et terra gloria tua.
Hosanna in excelsis.

Holy, holy, holy.
Lord God of Sabaoth!
Heaven and earth are full of thy glory!
Hosanna in the highest.

The Agnus Dei

Agnus Dei, qui tollis peccata mundi:
    miserere nobis.
Agnus Dei, qui tollis peccata mundi:
    miserere nobis.
Agnus Dei, qui tollis peccata mundi:
    dona nobis pacem.

O Lamb of God, that takest away the sins of the world,
    have mercy upon us.
O Lamb of God, that takest away the sins of the world,
    have mercy upon us.
O Lamb of God, that takest away the sins of the world,
    grant us thy peace.

[58]

The Words of Administration

The Body of our Lord Jesus Christ,
which was given for thee,
preserve thy body and soul unto everlasting life:
Take and eat this in remembrance that Christ died for thee,
and feed on him in thy heart by faith with thanksgiving.

The Blood of our Lord Jesus Christ,
which was shed for thee,
preserve thy body and soul unto everlasting life:
Drink this in remembrance that Christ's Blood was shed for thee,
and be thankful.

The Dismissal

Priest: Dominus vobiscum.   The Lord be with you.
All: Et cum spiritu tuo.   And with thy spirit.
Priest: Ite, missa est.   Go, the Mass is ended.
All: Deo gratias.   Thanks be to God.

5

Prayers for Morning

When day is come, why then come I
Simple in life's complexity,
To drink thy loveliness and pray
That I may walk the trodden way.

Anon.

O Lord our heavenly Father, Almighty and everlasting God,
who hast safely brought us to the beginning of this day:
Defend us in the same with thy mighty power;
and grant that this day we fall into no sin,
neither run into any kind of danger;
but that all our doings may be ordered by thy governance,
to do always that is righteous in thy sight;
through Jesus Christ our Lord.

The Third Collect, for Grace, from the Order for Morning Prayer

Into thy hands, O God,
We commend ourselves this day;
let thy presence be with us to its close.
Enable us to feel that in doing our work
we are doing thy will,
and that in serving others
we are serving thee.

Uppingham Prayer Book

O Lord, open thou our lips
And our mouth shall shew forth thy praise.

Grant, O Father, that this day
we may be doers of thy Word,
and not hearers only.

Remember, Christian soul,
that thou hast this day,
and every day of thy life,
God to glorify,
Jesus to imitate,
a soul to save,
a body to mortify,
sins to repent of,
virtues to acquire,
hell to avoid,
heaven to gain,
eternity to prepare for,
time to profit by,
neighbours to edify,
the world to despise,
devils to combat,
passions to subdue,
death perhaps to suffer,
judgement to undergo.

Now I arise, impow'r'd by Thee,
    The glorious sun to face;
O clothe me with humility,
    Adorn me with Thy grace.

O make me useful as I go
    My pilgrimage along;
And sweetly soothe this vale of woe
    By charity and song.

Let me from Christ obedience learn,
    To Christ obedience pay;
Each parent duteous love return
    And consecrate the day.

Christopher Smart, 1722–71, *At Dressing in the Morning*
A Prayer written for a little Prince, 1770

[64]

Lord Jesus Christ,
who alone art wisdom,
thou knowest what is best for us;
grant that it may happen to us only as it is pleasing to thee
and as it seems good in thy sight this day;
for thy Name's sake.

King Henry VI's *Prayer for the Day*

The Battle of Edgehill in 1642 was the first battle of the Civil War between
England's Royalist and Parliamentary forces. In a field, just before the attack,
Sir Jacob Asterley was on his knees. This is the prayer that he said:

O Lord, thou knowest how busy I must be this day.
If I forget Thee, do not Thou forget me . . .

Dear God, send me what you will good or bad, but give
me the strength to deal with it.

Maria Callas, 1923–77

Now another day is breaking,
Sleep was sweet and so is waking,
Dear Lord, I promised you last night
Never again to sulk or fight.
Such vows are easier to keep
When a child is sound asleep.
Today, O Lord, for your dear sake,
I'll try and keep them when awake.

Ogden Nash, 1902–71

To God the Father,
    who loved us, and made us accepted in the Beloved:
To God the Son,
    who loved us, and washed us from our sins by his own blood:
To God the Holy Ghost,
    who shed the love of God abroad in our hearts:
        To the one true God
        to be all love and glory
        for time and eternity.
Grant unto us, O Lord, this day
    to walk with thee as Father,
    to trust in thee as Saviour,
    to worship thee as Lord;
    that all our works may praise thee
    and our lives may give thee glory.

Anon.

And help us, this and every day,
To live more nearly as we pray.

John Keble, 1792–1866

6

Prayers for Evening

Nunc Dimittis

Lord, now lettest thou thy servant depart in peace:
    according to thy word.
For mine eyes have seen:
    thy salvation,
Which thou hast prepared:
    before the face of all people:
To be a light to lighten the Gentiles:
    and to be the glory of thy people Israel.
Glory be to the Father, and to the Son:
    and to the Holy Ghost;
As it was in the beginning, is now, and ever shall be:
    world without end. Amen.

The Order of Evening Service from *The Book of Common Prayer*:
The Gospel of Luke, 2:29–32

Lighten our darkness, we beseech thee, O Lord,
and by thy great mercy defend us from all perils and dangers
of this night; for the love of thy only Son, our Saviour,
Jesus Christ.

The Third Collect, for Aid against all Perils , from the Evening Service
in *The Book of Common Prayer*

Be present, O merciful God,
and protect us through the silent hours of this night,
so that we,
who are wearied by the changes and chances of this fleeting world,
may repose upon thy eternal changelessness;
through Jesus Christ our Lord.

From Compline (a monastic evening service)

Matthew, Mark, Luke, and John
Bless the bed that I lie on.
Before I lay me down to sleep
I give myself to Christ to keep.
Four corners to my bed,
Four Angels overspread:
One at the head, one at the feet,
And two to guard me while I sleep.
I go by sea, I go by land,
The Lord made me with his right hand.
If any danger come to me,
Sweet Jesus Christ, deliver me.
He is the branch and I'm the flower,
May God send me a happy hour.

A traditional prayer

Watch thou, dear Lord,
with those who wake or watch or weep tonight,
and give thine angels charge over those who sleep.
Tend thy sick ones, O Lord Christ,
Rest thy weary ones.
Bless thy dying ones,
Soothe thy suffering ones.
Pity thine afflicted ones.
Shield thy joyous ones.
And all for thy love's sake.

St Augustine, 345–430

Forgive me, Lord, for thy dear Son,
The ill that I this day have done,
That with the world, myself and thee,
I, ere I sleep, at peace may be.

Bishop Thomas Ken, 1637–1711

O Lord,
support us all the day long of this troublous life,
until the shadows lengthen and the evening comes,
and the busy world is hushed,
and the fever of life is over and our work is done.
Then, Lord, in thy mercy,
grant us a safe lodging, a holy rest,
and peace at the last.

Thought to be a sixteenth-century prayer
used by Cardinal Newman, 1801–90

Lord, let Your light be only for the day,
And the darkness for the night.
And let my dress, my poor humble dress
Lie quietly over my chair at night.

Let the church-bells be silent,
My neighbour Ivan not ring them at night.
Let the wind not waken the children
Out of their sleep at night.

Let the hen sleep on its roost, the horse in the stable
All through the night.
Remove the stone from the middle of the road
That the thief may not stumble at night.

Let heaven be quiet during the night.
Restrain the lightning, silence the thunder.
They should not frighten mothers giving birth
To their babies at night.

And me too protect against fire and water,
Protect my poor roof at night.
Let my dress, my poor humble dress
Lie quietly over my chair at night.

Nathan Bomze, 1906–54, a Yiddish poet

[71]

Close now thine eyes, and rest secure;
Thy soul is safe enough, thy body sure;
    He that loves thee, He that keeps
And guards thee, never slumbers, never sleeps.
The smiling Conscience in a sleeping breast
        Has only peace, has only rest:
        The music and the mirth of kings
Are all but discords, when she sings;
        Then close thine eyes and rest secure;
No sleep so sweet as thine, no rest so sure.

Francis Quarles, 1592–1644

We will lay us down in peace and take our rest;
For it is thou, Lord, only that makest us dwell in safety.

From Compline

Prayers for Special Days

There are special prayers for every Sunday of the year, for the day of every major saint, and for all important Church festivals.

A Sabbath Prayer

Lord of all creation,
You have made us the masters of Your world,
to tend it, to serve it, and to enjoy it.
For six days we measure and we build,
we count and carry the real and the imagined burdens of our task,
the success we earn and the price we pay.
On this day, the Sabbath day, give us rest.
For six days, if we are weary or bruised by the world,
if we think ourselves giants or cause others pain,
there is never a moment to pause, and know what we should really be.
On this day, the Sabbath day, give us time.
For six days we are torn between our private greed and the urgent needs of others,
between the foolish noises in our ears and the silent prayer of our soul.
On this day, the Sabbath day, give us understanding and peace.
Help us, Lord,
to carry these lessons, of rest and time, of understanding and peace,
into the six days that lie ahead, to bless us in the working days of our lives.

Jewish prayer

A Prayer for the New Year

Give us the will, O God,
to pray to thee continually,
to learn to know thee rightfully,
to serve thee always holily,
to ask thee all things needfully,
to praise thee always worthily,
to love thee always steadfastly,
to ask thy mercy heartily,
to trust thee always faithfully,
to obey him always willingly,
to abide him always patiently,
to use thy neighbour honestly,
to live here always virtuously,
to help the poor in misery,
to thank thee ever gratefully,
to hope for Heaven's felicity,
and to have faith, hope and charity.

Thomas Tusser, c. 1524–80

Easter

Most glorious Lord of Life! that, on this day,
Didst make Thy triumph over death and sin;
And, having harrowed hell, didst bring away
Captivity, thence captive, us to win;
This joyous day, dear Lord, with joy begin;
And grant that we, for who thou diddest die,
Being with Thy dear blood clean washed from sin,
May live for ever in felicity!
And that Thy love we weighing worthily,
May likewise love Thee for the same again;
And for Thy sake, that all like dear didst buy,
With love may one another entertain!
    So let us love, dear Love, like as we ought,
    – Love is the lesson which the Lord us taught.

Edmund Spenser, c. 1552–99

O Christmas Christ

Blessed art Thou, O Christmas Christ,
that Thy cradle was so low that Shepherds,
poorest and simplest of all earthly folk,
could yet kneel beside it,
and look level-eyed into the face of God.

Blessed art Thou,
that Thy cradle was so high that the Magi,
lords of learning and wealth,
could yet come to it by a Star's pathway,
to hazard their wisdom's store into Thy Baby hands.

Blessed art Thou that,
being grown to manhood, and being a carpenter,
Thou didst fashion a Christmas altar, like unto Thy cradle,
so that all simplicity and wisdom,
all poverty and wealth,
all righteousness and penitence for sin,
might find sanctuary there.

Be this our Christmas haste, O Christmas Christ,
to seek that altar, and,
at this season of Thy birth,
unafraid of the Time's complaint,
may we be found kneeling still.

Anon.

Collects

A 'collect' is a short prayer adapted to a particular occasion. It has a recognisable rhythm and pattern. There is no certain explanation for the name. Often a collect collects together in a prayer the meaning of the Epistle and Gospel readings for the day. It has also been suggested that on excursions from church to church, when all the people were collected together, a collect was said before they moved on to the next church. The collects in this section are from the Book of Common Prayer.

Blessed Lord,
who hast caused all holy Scriptures
to be written for our learning;
Grant that we may in such wise hear them,
read, mark, learn and inwardly digest them,
that by patience,
and comfort of thy holy Word,
we may embrace and ever hold fast
the blessed hope of everlasting life,
which thou hast given us in our Saviour Jesus Christ.

The Second Sunday in Advent

O Lord,
who hast taught us
that all our doings without charity are nothing worth;
Send thy Holy Ghost,
and pour into our hearts that most excellent gift of charity,
the very bond of peace and of all virtues,
without which whosoever liveth is counted dead before thee:
Grant this for thine only Son Jesus Christ's sake.

Quinquagesima Sunday

Almighty and everlasting God,
who, of thy tender love towards mankind,
hast sent thy Son our Saviour Jesus Christ,
to take upon him our flesh,
and to suffer death upon the cross,
that all mankind should follow the example of his great humility:
Mercifully grant,
that we may both follow the example of his patience,
and also be made partakers of his resurrection;
through the same Jesus Christ our Lord.

Palm Sunday, the Sunday next before Easter

O Almighty God,
    who alone canst order
the unruly wills and affections of sinful men;
Grant unto thy people,
that they may love the thing which thou commandest,
and desire that which thou dost promise;
that so,
among the sundry and manifold changes of the world,
our hearts may surely there be fixed,
where true joys are to be found;
through Jesus Christ our Lord.

The Fourth Sunday after Easter

O God,
who hast prepared for them that love thee
such good things as pass man's understanding:
Pour into our hearts such love toward thee,
that we,
loving thee above all things,
may obtain thy promises,
which exceed all that we can desire;
through Jesus Christ our Lord.

The Sixth Sunday after Trinity

Short Prayers

A short prayer finds its way to Heaven.

William Langland, c. 1330–1400

Speak, Lord, for thy servant heareth.

The First Book of Samuel, 3:9

Grant us grace, Almighty Father,
So to pray as to deserve to be heard.

Jane Austen, 1775–1817

O Lord never suffer us to think that we can stand by ourselves,
    and not need thee.

John Donne, 1572–1631

Jesus, strengthen my desire to work and speak and think for thee.

Charles Wesley, 1707–88

I ask not to see; I ask not to know; I ask only to be used.

Cardinal Newman, 1801–90

O Lord, let me not live to be useless.

John Wesley, 1703–91

O God, help us not to despise or oppose what we do not
understand.

William Penn, 1644–1718

Oh, Great Spirit, help me never to judge another until I have
walked two weeks in his moccasins.

A Sioux Indian prayer

Mark me like the tulip with thine own streaks.

Jami, 1414–91, a Sufi Prayer

Change the world, O Lord, beginning with me.

A Chinese student

O Lord, baptize our hearts into a sense of the conditions and
needs of all men.

George Fox, 1624–91

Lord, give us faith that right makes might.

Abraham Lincoln, 1809–65

God deliver us from sullen saints!

St Teresa of Avila, 1515–82

O God, I thank thee for all the joy I have had in life.

Earl Brihtnoth, d. 991A.D.

Lord, grant that my last hour may be my best hour.

A prayer recorded by John Aubrey, 1626–97

He, Ram! He, Ram! (Ah, God! Ah, God!)

Last words of Gandhi, 1869–1948

O my Father, if it be possible, let this cup pass from me;
    nevertheless not as I will, but as thou wilt.

Jesus of Nazareth

Lord, help me.

The Gospel of Matthew, 15:25

Prayers for Animals

A righteous man regardeth the life of his beast.

Book of Proverbs, 12:10

He prayeth well who loveth well
Both man and bird and beast;
He prayeth best, who loveth best
All things both great and small;
For the dear God who loveth us,
He made and loveth all.

Samuel Taylor Coleridge, 1772–1834,
The Ancient Mariner

Please God, take care of little things,
The fledglings that have not their wings,
Till they are big enough to fly
And stretch their wings across the sky.
Take care of small new lambs that bleat,
Small foals that totter on their feet,
And all small creatures ever known
Till they are strong to stand alone.

Eleanor Farjeon, 1881–1965, *A Prayer for Little Things*

Little things, that run, and quail,
And die, in silence and despair!

Little things, that fight, and fail,
And fall, on sea, and earth, and air!

All trapped and frightened little things,
The mouse, the coney, hear our prayer!

As we forgive those done to us,
– The lamb, the linnet, and the hare –

Forgive us all our trespasses,
Little creatures, everywhere.

James Stephens, 1882–1950

[89]

To all the humble beasts there be,
To all the birds on land and sea,
Great Spirit! sweet protection give,
That free and happy they may live!

And to our hearts the rapture bring
Of love for every living thing;
Make of us all one kin, and bless
Our ways with Christ's own gentleness!

John Galsworthy, 1867–1933

Hear our humble prayer, O God,
for our friends the animals,
especially for animals who are suffering;
for all that are overworked and underfed and cruelly treated;
for all wistful creatures in captivity that beat against their bars;
for any that are hunted or lost or deserted or frightened or hungry;
for all that are in pain or dying;
for all that must be put to death.
We entreat for them all thy mercy and pity,
and we ask for those who deal with them
a heart of compassion and gentle hands and kindly words.
Make us ourselves to be true friends to animals
and so to share the blessing of the merciful.
For the sake of thy Son the tender-hearted, Jesus Christ our Lord.

A Russian prayer

O ye Whales, and all that move in the Waters, bless ye the Lord:
    praise him, and magnify him for ever.
O all ye Fowls of the Air, bless ye the Lord:
    praise him, and magnify him for ever.
O all ye Beasts, and Cattle, bless ye the Lord:
    praise him, and magnify him for ever.

From the canticle *Benedicte, Omnia Opera* in *The Book of Common Prayer*

Thanksgiving and Praise

A single grateful thought raised to heaven
is the most perfect prayer.

Gotthold Ephraim Lessing, 1729–81

The General Thanksgiving

Almighty God, Father of all mercies,
>   we thine unworthy servants do give thee most humble and
>   hearty thanks for all thy goodness and loving-kindness
>   to us and to all men.
We bless thee
>   for our creation, preservation, and all the blessings
>   of this life; but above all
>   for thine inestimable love in the redemption of the world
>   by our Lord Jesus Christ,
>   for the means of grace, and for the hope of glory.
And we beseech thee,
>   give us that due sense of all thy mercies,
>   that our hearts may be unfeignedly thankful,
>   and that we shew forth thy praise,
>   not only with our lips, but in our lives;
>   by giving up ourselves to thy service,
>   and by walking before thee in holiness and righteousness
>   all our days;
>   through Jesus Christ our Lord,
>   to whom with thee and the Holy Ghost be all honour and
>   glory,
>   world without end.

The Book of Common Prayer

The Collect for Thanksgiving Day in the United States of America

O most merciful Father,
who hast blessed the labours of the husbandman in the
returns of the fruits of the earth; we give thee humble
and hearty thanks for this thy bounty;
beseeching thee to continue thy loving-kindness to us,
that our land may still yield her increase,
to thy glory and our comfort;
through Jesus Christ our Lord.

The Book of Common Prayer according to the use of the
Protestant Episcopal Church

God's gifts so many a pleasure bring
That I may make a thanksgiving.
For eyes whereby I clearly see
The many lovely things there be;
For lungs to breathe the morning air,
For nose to smell its fragrance rare;
For tongue to taste the fruits that grow,
For birds that sing and flowers that blow;
For limbs to climb, and swim and run,
For skin to feel the cheerful sun;
For sun and moon and stars in heaven,
Whose gracious light is freely given;
The river where the green weed floats,
And where I sail my little boats;
The sea where I can bathe and play,
The sands where I can race all day;
The pigeons wheeling in the sun,
Who fly more quickly than I run;
The winds that sing as they rush by,
The clouds that race across the sky;
The pony that I sometimes ride,
The curly dog that runs beside;
The shelter of the shady woods,
Where I may spend my lonely moods;

The gabled house that is my home,
The garden where I love to roam,
And bless my parents, every day,
Though they be very far away,
Take thou my thanks, O God above,
For all these tokens of thy love.
And when I am a man, do thou
Make me as grateful then as now.

Richard Molesworth Dennis,
who died in the 1914–18 War: *A Boy's Thanksgiving*

I asked for knowledge – power to control things;
I was granted understanding – to learn to love persons.

I asked for strength to be a Great Man;
I was made weak to become a better Man.

I asked for wealth to make friends;
I became poor, to keep friends.

I asked for all things to enjoy life;
I was granted all life, to enjoy things.

I cried for Pity; I was offered Sympathy.

I craved for healing of my own disorders;
I received insight into another's suffering.

I prayed to God for safety – to tread the trodden path;
I was granted danger, to lose track and find the Way.

I got nothing that I prayed for;
I am among all men, richly blessed.

Anon.

I thank thee, Lord,
for knowing me better than I know myself,
and for letting me know myself better than others know me.
Make me, I pray thee,
better than they suppose,
and forgive me what they do not know.

This prayer is attributed to Abu Bekr, c. 572–634. He was the father in-law
of Mohammed and the first Calif of Islam. The story goes that he said it when
he heard himself being praised.

The Magnificat

My soul doth magnify the Lord;
and my spirit hath rejoiced in God my Saviour.
For he hath regarded:
the lowliness of his hand-maiden.
For behold, from henceforth:
all generations shall call me blessed.
For he that is mighty hath magnified me:
and holy is his Name.
And his mercy is on them that fear him:
throughout all generations.
He hath showed strength with his arm:
he hath scattered the proud in the imagination of their hearts.
He hath put down the mighty from their seat:
and hath exalted the humble and meek.
He hath filled the hungry with good things:
and the rich he hath sent empty away.
He remembering his mercy hath holpen his servant Israel:
as he promised to our forefathers, Abraham and his seed, for ever.

The Order for Evening Service from *The Book of Common Prayer*; *The Gospel of Luke*
1:46–55

Ave Maria

Ave Maria,
gratia plena,
Dominus tecum;
benedicta tu in mulieribus,
et benedictus fructus ventris tui, Jesus.
Sancta Maria,
Mater Dei,
ora pro nobis peccatoribus,
nunc et in hora mortis nostrae. Amen.

Hail Mary, full of grace!
the Lord is with thee;
blessed art thou amongst women,
and blessed is the fruit of thy womb, Jesus.
Holy Mary, Mother of God,
pray for us sinners,
now and at the hour of our death.

The Daily Missal

Praise God from whom all blessings flow
Praise him, all creatures here below
Let all above the anthems raise
In one accord to sing his praise.

Bishop Thomas Ken, 1637–1711

The Song of the Creatures

O most high, almighty, good Lord God:
    to thee belong praise, glory, honour, and all blessing.
Praise be my Lord God, with all his creatures:
    and specially our brother the sun,
    who brings us the day and brings us the light.
Fair he is, and shiny with a very great splendour:
    O Lord, he signifies to us thee.

Praise be my Lord for all those who pardon one another for his love's sake:
    and who endure weakness and tribulation.
Blessed are they that peaceably shall endure:
    for thou, O most Highest, shalt give them a crown.
Praised be my Lord for our sister the death of the body:
    blessed are they who are found to be walking by thy most holy will.
Praise ye and bless ye the Lord and give thanks unto him:
    and serve him with great humility. Alleluya! Alleluya!

St Francis of Assisi, c. 1181–1226,
(translation by Matthew Arnold)

The Gloria

Gloria Patri,
et Filio,
et Spiritui Sancto.
Sicut erat in principio
et nunc et semper
et in saecula saeculorum.

Glory be to the Father,
and to the Son
and to the Holy Ghost;
As it was in the beginning,
is now, and ever shall be,
world without end.

Gloire au Père,
et au Fils,
et au Saint-Esprit.
Maintenant et toujours,
comme dès le commencement
et dans les siècles des siècles.

Graces

The word 'grace' comes from the Latin 'gratias' meaning thanks. The dictionary defines it as 'giving thanks for food', either before or after a meal, but graces may also be said on other occasions.

Graces before a Meal...and after

Come, God, be our guest;
May our food thus be blessed.

A prayer from Germany

For what we are about to receive
The Lord make us truly thankful.

Thank God for my good food.
Amen.

Benedictus benedicat, per Jesum Christum dominum nostrum.
May the blessed bless, through Jesus Christ our Lord.

Benedicto benedicatur.
Let the blessed be blessed.

Benedic, Domine,
nos et haec tua dona
quae de tua largitate
sumus sumpturi.

Bless us, O Lord,
and these thy gifts,
which of thy bounty
we are about to receive.

God bless our meat,
God guide our ways,
God give us grace our Lord to please.
Long preserve in peace and health
Our gracious Queen Elizabeth.

Written in the year of the Armada, 1588, by
George Bellin, an ironmonger of Exeter. It is
still widely used at City of London functions.

For food to eat, and those who prepare it,
For health to enjoy it, and friends to share it,
the Lord be praised.

Be present at our Table, Lord,
Be here and everywhere ador'd,
These creatures bless and grant that we
May feast in Paradise with thee.

Josiah Wedgwood gave John Wesley a teapot with this prayer on it.
The teapot was used by Wesley and his preachers and the grace became
popular amongst Methodists.

Here, a little child, I stand,
Heaving up my either hand:
Cold as paddocks though they be,
Here I lift them up to thee,
For a benison to fall
On our meat and on our all.

Robert Herrick, 1591–1674

What God gives, and what we take,
'Tis a gift for Christ his sake;
Be the meal of beans and pease,
God be thank'd for those, and these,
Have we flesh, or have we fish,
All are fragments of his dish.
He his Church save, and the king,
And our peace here, like a spring,
Make it ever flourishing.

Robert Herrick, 1591–1674

Heavenly Father, bless us
And keep us all alive,
There's ten of us to dinner,
And not enough for five.

Hodge's Grace, c. 1850

For every cup and plate full, God make us truly grateful.

Some ha'e meat, and canna eat,
And some would eat that want it;
But we ha'e meat, and we can eat,
And sae the Lord be thankit.

Robert Burns, 1759–96

Bless O Lord this food to our use and us in thy service, and keep us
mindful of the needs of others; for Christ's sake.

We have eaten and been satisfied. May we not be blind to the need of others, nor deaf to their cry for food. Open our eyes and our hearts so that we may share your gifts, and help to remove hunger and want from our world.

From a Jewish Thanksgiving after Meals

Give me a good digestion, Lord,
And also something to digest;
But when and how that something comes
I leave to thee, who knowest best.

Give me a healthy body, Lord;
Give me the sense to keep it so;
Also a heart that is not bored
Whatever work I have to do.

Give me a healthy mind, good Lord,
That finds the good that dodges sight;
And seeing sin, is not appalled,
But seeks a way to put it right.

Give me a point of view, good Lord,
Let me know what it is, and why,
Don't let me worry overmuch
About the thing that's known as 'I'.

Give me a sense of humour, Lord,
Give me the power to see a joke,
To get some happiness from life,
And pass it on to other folk.

Refectory Grace, Chester Cathedral,
written by Thomas Henry Basil Webb
when a boy at Winchester College.
He was killed on the Somme in 1917, aged nineteen.

Grace before Sleep

How can our minds and bodies be
Grateful enough that we have spent
Here in this generous room, we three,
This evening of content?
Each one of us has walked through storm
And fled the wolves along the road;
But here the hearth is wide and warm,
And for this shelter and this light
Accept, O Lord, our thanks tonight.

Sara Teasdale, 1884–1933

Lord, thou hast given so much to us, give one thing more,
a grateful heart; for Christ's sake.

Blessings

House Blessings

It is an old custom to have a house blessed
when people first move in

Unless the Lord builds the house,
its builders toil in vain.

Psalm 127, 1

God bless this house from thatch to floor,
The twelve apostles guard the door.
Four angels to my bed;
Gabriel stands at the head,
John and Peter at the feet,
All to watch me while I sleep.

A traditional blessing

God bless the master of this house
Likewise the mistress too,
And all the little children
That round the table go.

A traditional blessing

We ask His blessing on this home and all who live in it.
May its doors be open to those in need
and its rooms be filled with kindness.
May love dwell within its walls,
and joy shine from its windows.
May His peace protect it and His presence never leave it.

From a Jewish Service at Dedication of a Home

The beauty of this house is order;
the blessing of this house is contentment
the glory of this house is hospitality;
the crown of this house is peace.

Pax intrantibus
Salus exeuntibus
Benedicto habibantibus.

Peace to those entering
Health to those leaving
Blessings to those within.

God banish from your house
The fly, the roach, the mouse

That riots in the walls
Until the plaster falls;

Admonish from your door
The hypocrite and liar;

No shy, soft, tigrish fear
Permit upon your stair,

Nor agents of your doubt.
God drive them whistling out.

Stanley Kunitz, 1905 – , *Benediction*

Bless the four corners of this house,
    And be the lintel blessed,
And bless the hearth and bless the board,
    And bless each place of rest.
And bless the door which opens wide,
    To strangers as to kin,
And bless each crystal window pane
    That lets the sunshine in;
And bless the rooftree overhead,
    And every sturdy wall –
The peace of man, the peace of God,
    The peace of love on all.

Traditional

Touch the lintel and touch the wall,
Nothing but blessing here befall!
Bless the candle that stands by itself,
Bless the books on the mantel shelf.
Bless the hearth and the light it sheds,
Bless the pillow for tired heads.
Those who tarry here, let them know
A threefold blessing before they go:
Sleep for weariness – Peace for sorrow –
Faith in yesterday and tomorrow.
Those who go from here, let them bear
The blessing of hope wherever they fare.
Lintel and window, sill and wall,
Nothing but good this place befall.

Traditional

O God,
make the door of this house
wide enough to receive all who need human love and fellowship;
narrow enough to shut out all envy, pride and strife.
Make its threshold smooth enough to be no stumbling-block to children,
nor to straying feet,
but rugged and strong enough to turn back the tempter's power.
God make the door of this house
the gateway to thine eternal kingdom.

From the Church of St Stephen, Walbrook

Visit, we beseech thee, O Lord, this place,
and drive far from it all the snares of the enemy;
let thy holy angels dwell therein to preserve us in peace;
and may thy blessing be upon us evermore;
through Jesus Christ our Lord.

From Compline

God bless us, everyone

Tiny Tim, from Charles Dickens' *A Christmas Carol*

God's peace to me, peace of mankind,
And Saint Columba's peace, the kind,
Mild Mary's peace, a loving thing,
And peace of Christ the tender King,
    The peace of Christ the tender King,

Be on each window, on each door,
Each cranny-light upon the floor,
On house four corners may it fall,
And on my bed's four corners all,
    Upon my bed's four corners all;

Upon each thing mine eye doth see,
Upon each food that enters me,
Upon my body of the earth,
And on my soul of heavenly birth,
    Upon my body of the earth
    Upon my soul of heavenly birth.

A Gaelic blessing

Jesus Christ, Thou child so wise,
Bless mine hands and fill mine eyes,
And bring my soul to Paradise.

Hilaire Belloc, 1870–1953

God bless all those that I love;
God bless all those that love me.
God bless all those that love those that I love
And all those that love those that love me.

From an old New England sampler

Bless all who worship thee,
From the rising of the sun
Unto the going down of the same.
Of thy goodness, give us;
With thy love, inspire us;
By thy spirit, guide us;
By thy power, protect us;
In thy mercy, receive us,
Now and always.

Fifth-century prayer

The peace of God, which passeth all understanding,
keep your hearts and minds in the knowledge and love of God
and of his Son Jesus Christ our Lord:
And the Blessing of God Almighty, the Father, the Son
and the Holy Ghost,
be amongst you and remain with you always. Amen.

From the Order for Holy Communion in *The Book of Common Prayer*

Go forth into the world in peace;
　be of good courage;
　hold fast to that which is good;
　render to no man evil for evil;
　help the afflicted,
　honour all men;
　love and serve the Lord,
　rejoicing in the power of the Holy Spirit.
And the blessing of God Almighty, the Father, the Son and the
　Holy Ghost, be upon you and remain with you for ever.

The Book of Common Prayer, 1928

ACKNOWLEDGEMENTS

The publishers are indebted to the following for the use of copyright material: the lines from *The Birds* by Hilaire Belloc, published by Gerald Duckworth & Co. Ltd. and in the United States by Alfred A. Knopf Inc. are reprinted by permission of A.D. Peters & Co. Ltd; George Weidenfeld & Nicolson Ltd. for permission to include a prayer of Maria Callas; Michael Joseph for permission to include lines from *A Prayer for Little Things* from *Silver-Sand and Snow* by Eleanor Farjeon; the Society of Authors as the literary representative of the Estate of John Galsworthy for permission to include lines from John Galsworthy's poem *To all the humble beasts there be*; the National Trust and Macmillan London Ltd. for permission to reprint a verse from the poem, *The Children's Song* by Rudyard Kipling from *Puck of Pook's Hill*; Martin Secker & Warburg Ltd. for permission to include lines from *Benediction* by Stanley Kunitz from *The Poems of Stanley Kunitz 1928–1978* published in the United States by Little Brown and Company, Copyright 1930 by Stanley Kunitz; the Society of Authors as the literary representative of the Estate of John Masefield for permission to include lines from *The Everlasting Mercy* from *Poems* by John Masefield and in the United States reprinted with permission of Macmillan Publishing Co. Inc. Copyright 1912 by Macmillan Publishing Co. Inc. renewed 1940 by John Masefield; *Morning Prayer* by Ogden Nash from *The New Nutcracker Suite* is reprinted by permission of Curtis Brown Ltd. London, on behalf of the Estate of Ogden Nash and in the United States by permission of Curtis Brown Ltd., New York. Copyright 1961, 1962 by Ogden Nash; the prayer by Reinhold Niebuhr is included by permission of Ursula M. Niebuhr, Executor of the Literary Estate of Reinhold Niebuhr; the Society of Authors on behalf of the copyright owner, Mrs. Iris Wise, for permission to include an extract from *Little Things* from *Collected Poems* by James Stephens. Reprinted in the United States with permission of Macmillan Publishing Co. Inc., Copyright 1926 by Macmillan Publishing Co. Inc., renewed 1954 by Cynthia Stephens; Macmillan, London and Basingstoke for permission to include lines from two prayers by Rabindranath Tagore from *Collected Poems and Plays*. Reprinted in the United States with permission of Macmillan Publishing Co. Inc., lines from *Fruit-Gathering* from *Collected Poems and Plays* Copyright 1916 by Macmillan Publishing Co. Inc., renewed 1944 by Rabindranath Tagore and from *Gitanjali* by Rabindranath Tagore (New York: Macmillan 1913); the Macmillan Publishing Co. Inc., for permission to reprint lines from *Grace before Sleep* from *Collected Poems* by Sara Teasdale, Copyright 1932 by Macmillan Publishing Co. Inc., renewed 1961 by Guaranty Trust Co. of New York Exr.

Extracts from *The Book of Common Prayer* of 1662 which is Crown Copyright, are reproduced by permission.

Every effort has been made to trace holders of copyright material. If, however, any query should arise it should be addressed to the Publishers.

INDEX